KAMEHAMEHA THE GREAT

Revised Edition

Julie Stewart Williams

Illustrated by
Robin Yoko Burningham

Kamehameha Schools/Bernice Pauahi Bishop Estate

Community Education Division
Intermediate Reading Program

Honolulu, Hawai'i
1993

KAMEHAMEHA SCHOOLS/BERNICE PAUAHI BISHOP ESTATE

Board of Trustees
Myron B. Thompson, Chairman
Oswald K. Stender, 1st Vice Chairman
Richard S.H. Wong, 2nd Vice Chairman
Lokelani Lindsey, Secretary
Henry H. Peters, Treasurer

Administration
Michael J. Chun, Ph.D., President
Fred Cachola, Director, Community Education Division
Julie S. Williams, Director
Kamehameha Schools Intermediate Reading Program

*Cover portrait, "Kamehameha, King of the Sandwich Islands,"
a watercolor by Louis Choris,
courtesy of the Honolulu Academy of Arts*

Dedication

To my dear friend and cousin,

Violet-Marie Mahela Awai Rosehill,

master teacher of music,

Hawaiian culture and history and

my partner in the development of

instructional materials for children.

Table of Contents

Preface ix

Acknowledgments xi

Introduction 1

Kamehameha, the Child (1758–1763)

Pai‘ea 4

A Secret Beginning 5

Nae‘ole, his *Kahu* 12

Named Kamehameha 15

Kamehameha, the Student (1763–1775)

Training for Leadership 18

Games 20

Kalani‘ōpu‘u, his Uncle 24

Kekūhaupi‘o, his Teacher 26

Kōnane 32

Water Sports. 34

A Warrior in Training 38

Kamehameha, the Warrior (1775–1796)

1775: First Battle. 44

The Naha Stone 46

Visits with Captain Cook 48

Custody of the War God 52

The Chiefs of Kona 54

1782: The Battle of Moku'ōhai. 56

A Great Warrior Dies. 58

The Splintered Paddle. 58

Ka'ahumanu, his Favorite Wife 60

Young and Davis, his Friends. 62

1790: The Battle of Kepaniwai. 64

A *Heiau* for Kūkā'ilimoku 66

Wars with Keōua 68

Favored by Pele 69

1791: Chief of his Island 71

Vancouver, his Friend 74

More Islands. 75

1795: The Battle of Nu'uanu 76

Keōpūolani, his Sacred Wife. 77

Kaua'i 80

Revolt in Hilo 82

Kamehameha, the Chief (1796–1819)

The Chief Rules. 84

Law of the Splintered Paddle 86

Gifts for Pele 88

A Year in Lahaina. 90

1810: All the Islands United 91

Return to the Island of Hawai'i 93

Kamakahonu, his Last Home 96

The Hawaiian Flag. 102

Visits by Russian Ships 104

Last Words 109

A Secret Burial 110

The Greatest of Chiefs 111

"Kamehameha, King of the Sandwich Islands" 112

The King Kamehameha Memorial Statue 114

Kamehameha: A Name Chant 116

Bibliography. 119

Preface

This book is one of a series written for Kamehameha Schools Intermediate Reading Program (KSIRP) students. They are designed to increase students' reading skills and their knowledge of Hawaiian history and culture by focusing on topics such as the Hawaiian monarchy.

The books are written by KSIRP staff in an effort to provide young readers with culturally relevant materials in language arts and Hawaiian studies. The authors are pleased that the books have been well received by both educational and general audiences.

KSIRP is a Community Education Division program of Kamehameha Schools/Bernice Pauahi Bishop Estate. It is operated in collaboration with the State of Hawai'i Department of Education at several intermediate schools throughout the state.

Michael J. Chun, Ph.D.
President
Kamehameha Schools

Acknowledgments

I am indebted to those historians whose research provided valuable sources of information. I am very grateful to friends and colleagues whose *kōkua* made this book possible. *"Mahalo a nui loa"* to the late Dr. Donald D. Kilolani Mitchell who generously shared his knowledge on Kamehameha; to Robin Yoko Burningham whose vivid illustrations enhance the young reader's understanding of the text; to Mahela Rosehill, Paula DeMorales and Nalani Sing who provided their expertise for the first edition of the text written in 1985 for the student booklet *Explore the Island of Hawai'i;* to Marsha Bolson and Lesley Agard who reviewed the manuscript for clarity of thought and expression; to Nu'ulani Atkins who assisted in the preparation of the first edition; and to Russell Kawika Makanani who critiqued this edition for historical and cultural accuracy and shared his knowledge and valuable insights. *Mahalo* and a fond *aloha* to the late Keoni DuPont who ensured the proper use of Hawaiian.

J.S.W.

"Kamehameha in Red Vest,"
by Louis Choris (1816)
Portrait courtesy of Honolulu Academy of Arts

Introduction

Kamehameha was born in secret and buried in secret. In between he lived a very public life of action, courage, wisdom and justice. He brought together the smaller separate island chiefdoms, uniting them into one great Hawaiian nation. Under his later leadership people lived peaceful and productive lives.

Kamehameha the Great was written to tell young readers about the first ruler of all Hawai'i. It is based upon traditional and historical sources including writings by people who lived at that time and oral histories handed down over the last two centuries.

Many questions remain and historical debate continues concerning specific events of Kamehameha's life. No one now or in the future will ever know all the true details. This version contains selected highlights of commonly accepted accounts portraying events and personal characteristics which helped Kamehameha become known as the greatest of all Hawaiians.

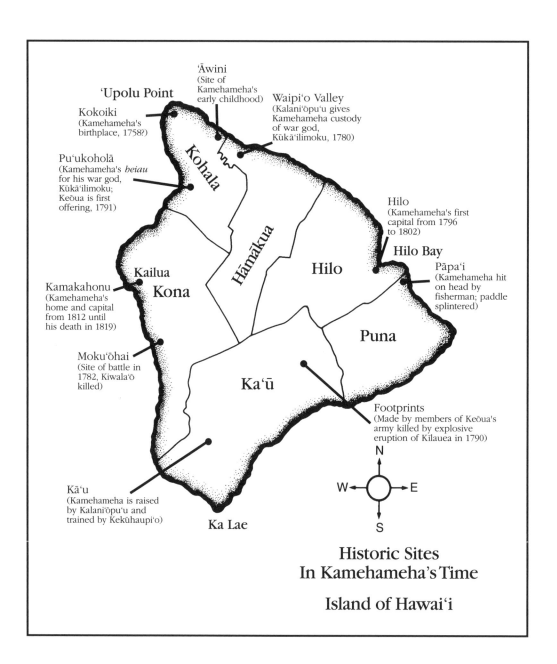

'Upolu Point

'Āwini
(Site of Kamehameha's early childhood)

Kokoiki
(Kamehameha's birthplace, 1758?)

Waipi'o Valley
(Kalani'ōpu'u gives Kamehameha custody of war god, Kūkā'ilimoku, 1780)

Pu'ukoholā
(Kamehameha's *heiau* for his war god, Kūkā'ilimoku; Keōua is first offering, 1791)

Kohala

Hāmākua

Hilo
(Kamehameha's first capital from 1796 to 1802)

Hilo Bay

Hilo

Pāpa'i
(Kamehameha hit on head by fisherman; paddle splintered)

Kailua

Kona

Kamakahonu
(Kamehameha's home and capital from 1812 until his death in 1819)

Moku'ōhai
(Site of battle in 1782, Kiwala'ō killed)

Puna

Ka'ū

Footprints
(Made by members of Keōua's army killed by explosive eruption of Kilauea in 1790)

Kā'u
(Kamehameha is raised by Kalani'ōpu'u and trained by Kekūhaupi'o)

Ka Lae

N
W — E
S

Historic Sites In Kamehameha's Time

Island of Hawai'i

2

Kamehameha, the Child

(1758–1763)

Pai'ea

Thunder and lightning,
Cold wind and rain;
A comet shines above
Kohala!
Kohala!

The cry of a babe
Born on this night,
A royal son, called
Pai'ea!
Pai'ea!

A Secret Beginning

Kamehameha was born on a stormy night at Kokoiki in Kohala, on the island of Hawai'i. Exactly when he was born is not known. It may have been in November, for November is the month of rain, thunder and lightning.

A bright star with a long tail appeared during Kamehameha's birth. That kind of star is a comet. Astronomers know that Halley's comet was seen in 1758. It is probable that Kamehameha was born in November 1758.

Kamehameha's mother was the young chiefess Keku'iapoiwa. As soon as Kamehameha was born Keku'iapoiwa wrapped him in *kapa* and placed him gently in the arms of Nae'ole, a chief of Kohala whom she trusted. "Take my child to my cousin Kaha'ōpulani! Go quickly!"

Nae'ole held the child close to him and ran as fast as he could to a secret place in 'Āwini, Kohala. Kaha'ōpulani was waiting for him in a cave. When Nae'ole arrived she took the baby and laid him on a mat. She covered the child with light fibers of *olonā*. Then she picked up her own baby girl and rocked her in her arms. The little boy was sleeping soundly.

Chief Nae'ole ran quickly with the baby

Keku'iapoiwa had planned for the safety of her baby. She knew that her uncle Alapa'inui did not want her child to live. Alapa'inui was the *ali'i nui,* or ruling chief, of the island of Hawai'i. A *kahuna,* or priest, had warned him that the child would grow up to be a mighty ruler and would conquer him. Alapa'inui did not want that to happen. He ordered his warriors to search for the baby.

Before long warriors entered Kaha'ōpulani's cave. They looked around for a baby boy. But the only baby they saw was the little girl in Kaha'ōpulani's arms. They did not see the baby that was fast asleep under the *olonā* fibers. The warriors hurried away.

A kahuna warned Alapaʻinui about the baby

The child was safe! Kahaʻōpulani was very happy. She loved the little boy and cared for him as if he were her own son. He was called Paiʻea, which means "hard-shelled crab." Paiʻea spent the next five years in ʻĀwini with his foster mother Kahaʻōpulani, her daughter and the chief who carried him to safety, Naeʻole.

Kahaʻōpulani and Paiʻea

Nae'ole, his *Kahu*

Nae'ole was Pai'ea's *kahu*. A *kahu* is a guardian, an attendant and a tutor. Nae'ole knew that the young chief must have the proper training. He raised Pai'ea in 'Āwini with great care. He taught him to swim while he was still a baby. It was said that Pai'ea could swim long before he could walk.

Naeʻole taught Paiʻea to swim

Kamehameha at the age of five

Named Kamehameha

When Pai'ea was five years old Nae'ole returned him to his parents, Chief Keōuakupuapāikalaninui and Chiefess Keku'iapoiwa. They lived in Kailua-Kona, in the royal court of Alapa'inui. They wanted their son to live there too.

Alapa'inui welcomed the young boy. No longer was he fearful of the *kahuna's* warning about the child. Instead he gave Pai'ea the title of chief and named him Kamehameha, which means "The Lonely One."

Kamehameha returned to his parents

Kamehameha, the Student

(1763–1775)

Training for leadership

*F*rom earliest childhood young chiefs like Kamehameha were trained for leadership. Those who excelled in every way became great leaders.

Nae'ole was both careful and strict in training Kamehameha. He taught Kamehameha the knowledge, traditions and skills young chiefs needed to know. Kamehameha learned many things and had to be able to practice those skills he learned.

Genealogical chants showed how the young chief was related to the gods. Kamehameha had to memorize all the names of his ancestors. He had to know the great deeds performed by each ancestor.

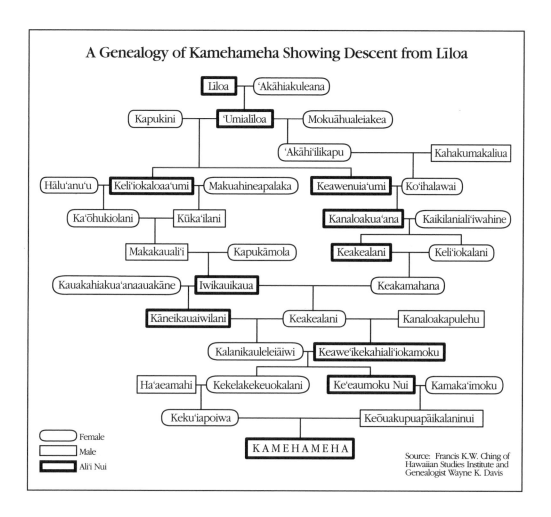

A Genealogy of Kamehameha Showing Descent from Līloa

Līloa — ʻAkāhiakuleana

Kapukini — ʻUmialīloa — Mokuāhualeiakea

ʻAkāhiʻilikapu — Kahakumakaliua

Hāluʻanuʻu — Keliʻiokaloaaʻumi — Makuahineapalaka   Keawenuiaʻumi — Koʻihalawai

Kaʻōhukiolani — Kūkaʻilani   Kanaloakuaʻana — Kaikilanialiʻiwahine

Makakaualiʻi — Kapukāmola   Keakealani — Keliʻiokalani

Kauakahiakuaʻanaauakāne — Iwikauikaua   Keakamahana

Kāneikauaiwilani — Keakealani — Kanaloakapulehu

Kalanikauleleiāiwi — Keaweʻīkekahialiʻiokamoku

Haʻaeamahi — Kekelakekeuokalani   Keʻeaumoku Nui — Kamakaʻimoku

Kekuʻiapoiwa — Keōuakupuapāikalaninui

KAMEHAMEHA

Female
Male
Aliʻi Nui

Source: Francis K.W. Ching of
Hawaiian Studies Institute and
Genealogist Wayne K. Davis

19

Games

$\mathscr{L}$earning many different games was an important part of Kamehameha's training. The more he practiced the stronger and more skillful he became.

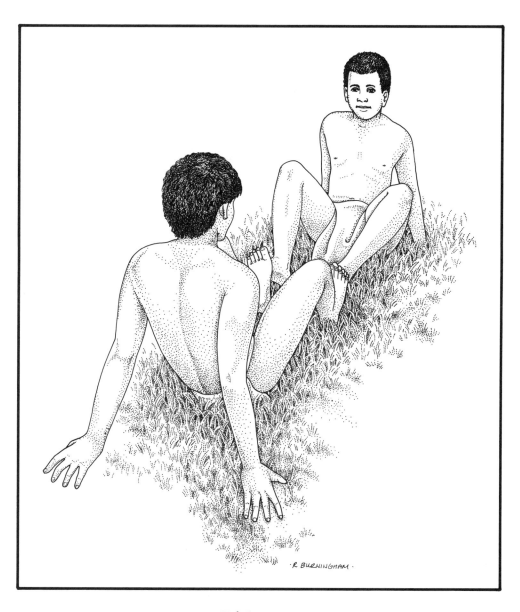

Kulaʻi wāwae
Foot pushing

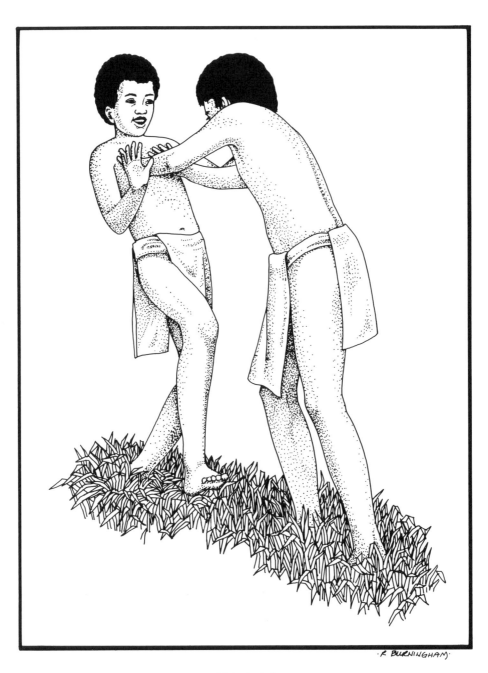

Kula kula'i
Chest pushing

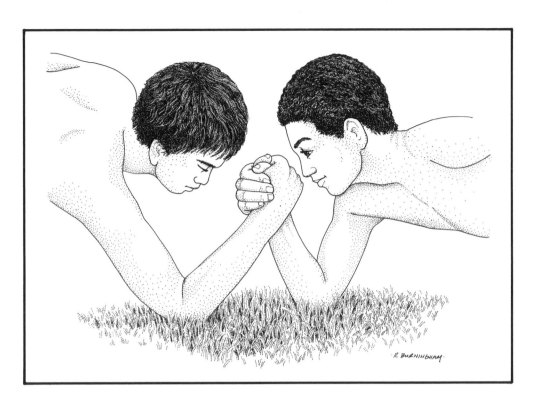

Uma
Hand wrestling

Kalaniʻōpuʻu, his Uncle

When Kamehameha was about twelve years old Keōua, his father, became very ill. Keōua asked his older brother Kalaniʻōpuʻu, Kamehameha's uncle, to take care of Kamehameha. Keōua wanted Kamehameha to be brought up by someone who would know what was best for him.

After Keōua died Kalaniʻōpuʻu took Kamehameha to his home in Kaʻū. There he raised the young chief as his own son.

·R BURNINGHAM·

Kalaniʻōpuʻu and Kamehameha

Kekūhaupiʻo, his Teacher

Kalaniʻōpuʻu chose Kekūhaupiʻo to be Kamehameha's teacher. Kekūhaupiʻo was the greatest warrior of that time. Alone he would step out and challenge an entire army. He once brought victory to his side by beating an enemy warrior in a contest. In this contest he dodged three stones as they were hurled at him from a fiber sling.

Kekūhaupiʻo continued Kamehameha's training in vigorous sports. Sports taught the young student to endure, or bear, that which is difficult. Sports helped him to develop courage.

These games required Kamehameha to concentrate, or keep his mind on what he was doing and work hard. He practiced and did not give up.

Kekūhaupiʻo taught Kamehameha that which he needed to know to be a successful warrior and chief. Besides being Kamehameha's teacher Kekūhaupiʻo was also his counselor and companion.

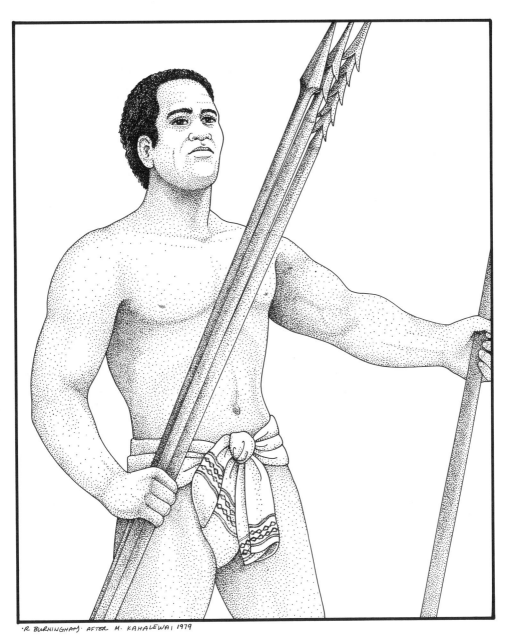

The great warrior Kekūhaupiʻo

He‘e hōlua
Sledding

Kūpololū

Pole vaulting

'Ulu Maika
Rolling stone discs

Hākōkō
Hawaiian wrestling

Kōnane

Kamehameha excelled at active games but he also learned quiet games. He became a champion player of *kōnane,* or Hawaiian checkers. He would spend long hours at a time playing *kōnane.* No one could beat him.

Kōnane
Hawaiian checkers

Water Sports

Kamehameha was outstanding at water sports including canoeing, surfing and swimming.

Kamehameha was a healthy person. He ate nutritious food and exercised daily playing different games and sports. Others described him as having a perfect body and well-formed features.

Heihei waʻa
Canoe racing

He'e nalu
Surfing

'Au

Swimming

A Warrior in Training

Kamehameha's teen-age years were spent training as a warrior. Warrior training used combat tactics while playing games fighting in sham, or imitation, battles.

Kekūhaupiʻo taught Kamehameha the arts of warfare. He trained the young warrior in hand-to-hand fighting. He taught him how to throw, thrust, catch, dodge and parry, or turn aside, spears.

Kamehameha became the most skillful of all the chiefs in the use of the spear. Captain George Vancouver later wrote that he once saw six spears hurled at Kamehameha all at the same time. Kamehameha caught three with one hand as they flew at him. Two he broke by hitting them with a spear in his other hand. One he dodged.

Kākā lāʻau
Fencing with spears

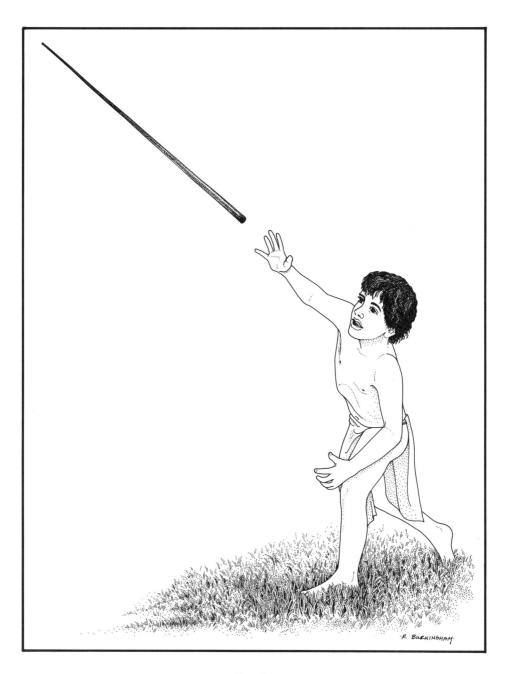

'Ō'ō ihe
Spear throwing

40

Kamehameha learned the rules of warfare practiced in Hawai'i. One rule, for example, was that special religious ceremonies had to take place before a war could start.

Knowing the code of ethics, or rules of moral duties, was important too. For instance it was considered wrong to attack an enemy without first warning him.

Kekūhaupi'o taught Kamehameha many things. The young chief learned how to perform his religious duties and ceremonies. He had lessons in astronomy, geography and navigation. He studied the winds and clouds. He watched the birds in flight. He learned the habits of fish. He memorized long chants.

At the end of Kamehameha's training it was predicted, or foretold, that he would be a great warrior in all his battles. Kekūhaupiʻo would be killed in a sham battle, but Kamehameha would not even be injured. The prophecy, or prediction of future events, would come true.

Kamehameha, the Warrior

(1775–1796)

1775: First Battle

In his very first battle Kamehameha proved that he was a great warrior by saving the life of Kekūhaupiʻo, his teacher. The battle took place on Maui in 1775. Alapaʻinui had died. Kalaniʻōpuʻu, the new chief, was at war with Maui's Chief Kahekili. The battle was fought in a sweet potato field. It is said that Kekūhaupiʻo's feet were caught in the sweet potato vines and he fell. He would have been killed were it not for the quick action of his young pupil Kamehameha, who brought other warriors to his rescue.

Kamehameha saved the life of his teacher Kekūhaupiʻo

The Naha Stone

In 1775 high-ranking chiefs watched as the young Kamehameha proved that he was very strong. He overturned the Naha stone which weighed nearly five thousand pounds. According to prophecy he who overturned the Naha stone would conquer all of the islands.

The Naha stone now rests in front of the Hawai'i County Library in Hilo on Waiānuenue Avenue. This is near the site of Pinao, the ancient *heiau,* or place of worship. Next to the Naha stone is the entrance pillar of Pinao.

Kamehameha overturned the Naha stone

Visits with Captain Cook

The first known Western explorer to visit the Hawaiian islands was the English navigator Captain James Cook. Captain Cook arrived in January 1778. Although Oʻahu was sighted earlier, it was on Kauaʻi that he and his men first went ashore. On Kauaʻi they traded nails and bits of iron for water, pork, fish, sweet potatoes and *kalo*. On Niʻihau they traded for yams and salt. Two weeks later Cook's two ships, the *Resolution* and the *Discovery,* sailed off to the north.

In November 1778 Captain Cook returned to the islands. His ships anchored off the north coast of Maui. Kahekili, chief of Maui, visited the *Discovery* and gave Captain Charles Clerke a red feather cloak. A few days later the ships were off the east end of the island near Hāna. Kalaniʻōpuʻu was in Hāna at that time. He and his chiefs went aboard the *Resolution*. They visited with Captain Cook for two hours. Kamehameha and six other chiefs remained on board overnight.

Captain James Cook with the young chief Kamehameha

In January 1779 Captain Cook sailed to Kealakekua
Bay off the Kona coast of Hawai'i. Kalani'ōpu'u and
Kamehameha once again visited the English navigator.
One of Cook's men described Kamehameha as a
young man who seemed to be a favorite of the chief.
Kalani'ōpu'u gave Captain Cook several feather
cloaks. In return, Cook gave Kalani'ōpu'u a linen
shirt, a sword and later a tool chest.

Captain Cook's ship, the Resolution, *in Kealakekua Bay*

Custody of the War God

In 1780 Kalani'ōpu'u met with his chiefs in Waipi'o Valley. He told them what to do after his death. His oldest son Kiwala'ō was to be the new king. His younger son Keōua Kūahu'ula was to be given lands. His nephew Kamehameha was to be in charge of the war *heiau* and Kūkā'ilimoku, the family's feathered war god.

Kalaniʻōpuʻu met with his chiefs in Waipiʻo Valley

The Chiefs of Kona

Chief Kalaniʻōpuʻu died in Kaʻū in 1782. His son Kiwalaʻō was now the ruler of the island of Hawaiʻi. Kiwalaʻō divided up the lands. This led to trouble.

The chiefs of Kona were angry about the land division. They turned to Kamehameha for help. Kamehameha was living in Kohala at that time. He agreed to become their leader. The chiefs of Kona were:

- Keaweaheulu—uncle and counselor to Kamehameha;
- Keʻeaumoku—father of Kaʻahumanu;
- Kamanawa and Kameʻeiamoku—uncles of Kamehameha and twin brothers who are pictured on Hawaiʻi's coat of arms;
- Kekūhaupiʻo—the great warrior and teacher of Kamehameha; and
- Kalaʻimamahū, Kawelookalani and Keliʻimaikaʻi—Kamehameha's three brothers.

These chiefs remained loyal to Kamehameha as long as they lived.

UA MAU KE EA O KA AINA I KA PONO

·R.BURNINGHAM·

Hawaiʻi's coat of arms

1782:
The Battle of Moku'ōhai

*M*any chiefs did not like the way Kiwala'ō had divided the lands. This led to a battle which was fought in Ke'ei, Kona. It was called the battle of Moku'ōhai. Kiwala'ō was killed. He was wearing a feather cloak of yellow *'ō'ō* feathers with triangles of red *'i'iwi* feathers. Since Kamehameha won the battle the cloak belonged to him. Today this beautiful cloak is in Bishop Museum.

The island of Hawai'i was now split into three chiefdoms, each with its own ruler: (1) Kamehameha—ruler of Kona, Kohala and northern Hāmākua; (2) Keōua—ruler of Ka'ū and part of Puna; and (3) Keawema'uhili—ruler of Hilo and parts of Puna and Hāmākua.

For the next nine years Kamehameha tried but failed at conquering the rest of the island of Hawai'i.

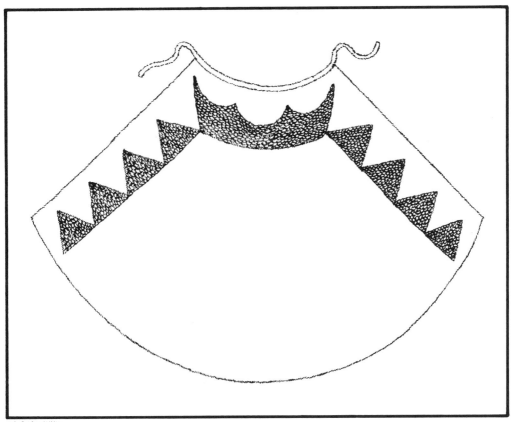

Kiwala'ō's feather cloak

A Great Warrior Dies

Kekūhaupiʻo died in Nāpōʻopoʻo in 1784 the way it had been foretold. He was struck by a spear during a sham battle.

The Splintered Paddle

One day, shortly after Kekūhaupiʻo's death, Kamehameha set out in a war canoe. As he sailed along the Puna coast he saw some fishermen on the beach at Pāpaʻi. They had something he wanted. Kamehameha jumped ashore to take it away from them but they ran away. While he was chasing them he slipped. His foot got stuck between the rocks.

One of the fishermen saw what happened and ran back. He lifted his paddle and struck Kamehameha on the head so hard that the paddle was splintered to pieces. The fisherman did not know that the man he hit was Kamehameha. He ran away. Kamehameha later freed his foot and went back to his canoe.

The fisherman struck Kamehameha and the paddle splintered

Ka'ahumanu,
his Favorite Wife

Ka'ahumanu was born in Hāna. Her father was Ke'eaumoku, trusted advisor to Kamehameha. Her mother was Nāmāhana, sister of Kahekili, the chief of Maui.

Kamehameha married Ka'ahumanu in 1785 when she was seventeen years old. Kamehameha had other wives but Ka'ahumanu was the wife he loved best of all. Ka'ahumanu spoke of Kamehameha in this *'ōlelo no'eau:*

"Pāpale 'ai 'āina, ku'u aloha."

"The head covering over the land, my beloved."

Ka'ahumanu

Young and Davis, his Friends

Many ships stopped at the islands to rest and to trade for supplies. From such ships came two Englishmen, John Young and Isaac Davis. Kamehameha saw that they were wise and honest. He added them to his staff of advisors and warriors.

Young and Davis helped Kamehameha by getting foreign weapons for him. They manned the cannons and guns during the battles. Kamehameha gave each of them a wife and lands. Later he made them chiefs.

John Young

1790:
The Battle of Kepaniwai

Kamehameha still could not conquer all of his own island of Hawai'i. In the summer of 1790 he headed for Maui and fought against Kalanikūpule, son of Kahekili. Kamehameha showed great skill in his use of military strategies. The fighting ended in 'Īao Valley. The waters of 'Īao Stream were dammed, or blocked, by the bodies of dead warriors. This battle became known as the battle of Kepaniwai which means "damming of the waters."

Kamehameha won the battle, and Kalanikūpule escaped to O'ahu. Kamehameha sent his warriors back to Hawai'i while he sailed to Moloka'i.

Ïao Valley, Maui

A *Heiau* for Kūkā'ilimoku

Kamehameha wanted to find out what he must do to conquer all the islands. From Moloka'i he sent a messenger to Kapoukahi, a Kaua'i *kahuna* who was living in Waikīkī. Kapoukahi said that Kamehameha must build a great new *heiau* for his war god Kūkā'ilimoku. The place for this *heiau* was Pu'ukoholā near Kawaihae on the island of Hawai'i. Only then could he conquer the islands without a scratch to his own skin.

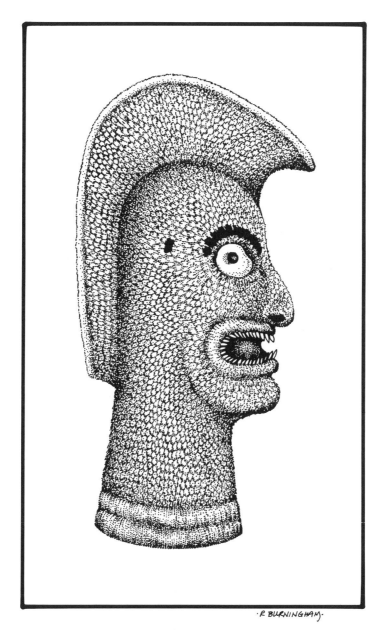

R BURNINGHAM

Kūkāʻilimoku

Wars with Keōua

Meanwhile on Hawai'i Keōua was plundering Kamehameha's lands in Waipi'o, Kohala and Waimea. He dried up the fishponds. He pulled up all the *kalo* plants in Waipi'o. He robbed and hurt Kamehameha's people.

Kamehameha loved his people. He said, "*Auē!* While I have been seeking new children my first-born have been abandoned!" He returned to his island.

Two battles were fought against Keōua in Hāmākua. Neither side won. Kamehameha went back to Waipi'o and Kohala.

Favored by Pele

Keōua started back to his own lands in Kaʻū. To get there he had to pass Kīlauea volcano. His people were in three groups. As the middle group neared the volcano it erupted. The eruption was explosive. Men, women and children were killed by lava chunks, ash and poisonous gases. Some of their footprints can still be seen in the hardened lava. This event took place in 1790 and was seen as a sign that Pele was on Kamehameha's side.

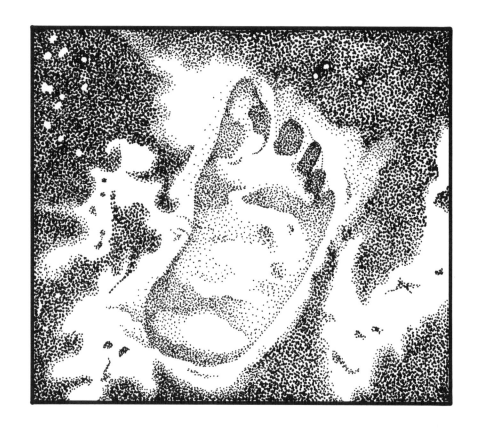

A footprint in the lava

1791: Chief of his Island

Kamehameha had tried to win his own island for nine years. Now he believed that only the gods could defeat Keōua. He decided to build the new *heiau* for his war god at Pu'ukoholā. When the *heiau* was finished he invited Keōua to talk with him about peace. Keōua agreed to see him.

Two large canoes filled with the highest chiefs of Ka'ū entered Kawaihae Bay. Keōua was in one canoe. The other canoe was led by a young chief named Ka'ōleiokū. Ka'ōleiokū was Kamehameha's son, his first child. Ka'ōleiokū's mother was Kānekapōlei, who was also Keōua's mother.

Keōua stepped ashore. As he did he was killed by a spear hurled by Keʻeaumoku. A great commotion took place and all who were with Keōua on his canoe were killed by Kamehameha's warriors. Did Kamehameha want this to happen? No one knows for sure.

Kamehameha stopped his men from harming those in the other canoe. In the other canoe was his son.

Keōua's body and those of his chiefs were offered as sacrifices on the altar of the new *heiau*. The whole island of Hawaiʻi was now under Kamehameha's rule.

Pu'ukoholā heiau

Vancouver, his Friend

English Captain George Vancouver revisited Hawai'i in 1792, 1793 and 1794. On all the islands he met important chiefs. As he traveled he was shocked by the destruction he saw from the many recent battles. He told the chiefs, including Kahekili and Kamehameha, it was better to live in peace with each other and visiting foreigners.

Vancouver now found Kamehameha to be less stern than fourteen years earlier and having "…an open, cheerful and sensible mind; combined with great generosity and goodness of disposition."

Vancouver brought cattle, sheep, grapevines, orange and almond trees and a variety of garden seeds to Hawai'i. While given to the Hawaiians to raise, these foods were also expected to benefit British seamen stopping in the islands.

More Islands

Kahekili, ruler of Maui and Oʻahu, died in 1794. Now was the right time for Kamehameha to fight for the other islands. He had a fleet of 960 canoes and 20 foreign ships. He had an army of sixteen thousand men.

In February 1795 Kamehameha conquered Maui, Molokaʻi and Lānaʻi. He then rested on Molokaʻi and made plans for the invasion of Oʻahu.

1795:
The Battle of Nuʻuanu

In April 1795 Kamehameha and his army sailed to Oʻahu. They landed on the shore from Waiʻalae to Waikīkī. They fought their way up Nuʻuanu Valley. Some Oʻahu warriors were driven over the Pali ("Cliff"). Chief Kalanikūpule of Oʻahu escaped but was captured a few months later.

Kamehameha won the battle of Nuʻuanu. He was now ruler of all the islands except Kauaʻi and Niʻihau.

Keōpūolani,
his Sacred Wife

After the battle of Nuʻuanu in 1795
Kamehameha married Keōpūolani, who was
just seventeen years old. Her grandmother Kalola had
promised her to Kamehameha in marriage when she
was about eleven. The name Keōpūolani means
"The Gathering of the Clouds of Heaven."

Keōpūolani was the highest ranking of
Kamehameha's wives. Her ancestors were of four
high-chiefly lines. Her father, Kiwalaʻō, was of the
family of high chiefs of the islands of Kauaʻi, Oʻahu,
Maui and Hawaiʻi. Her mother, Kekuʻiapoiwa Liliha,
was of the family of high chiefs of Maui and Hawaiʻi.
Because of her superior rank, Keōpūolani was raised
under many *kapu* as a sacred person.

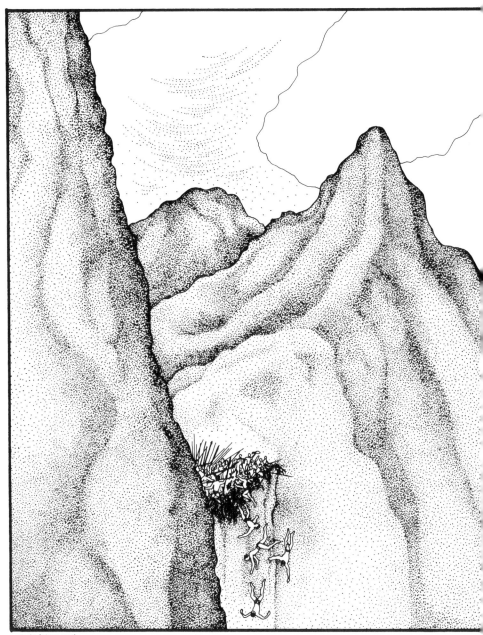

·R BURNINGHAM·

78

Nuʻuanu Pali, Oʻahu

Kaua'i

In the spring of 1796 Kamehameha set sail to conquer Kaua'i. He may have had more than eight hundred *peleleu* canoes. A *peleleu* canoe is a large, often double-hulled canoe. Strong winds and rough seas swamped many of Kamehameha's canoes. This forced him to postpone the invasion of Kaua'i.

Peleleu *canoe*

Revolt in Hilo

On September of 1796 Kamehameha went to Hilo to combat an uprising against his rule. This was his very last fight. After defeating his enemies he remained in Hilo for the next six years.

Kamehameha, the Chief

(1796–1819)

The Chief Rules

Hilo was capital of the kingdom for the six years between 1796 and 1802. Kamehameha organized his government by first chosing a governor for each island. He made laws to protect both chiefs and commoners. He had rules for fishing. He encouraged the people to raise food. He chose craftsmen to make needed items.

Everyone had to work. The chief himself worked hard with his own hands.

Trading with foreign ships grew. Kamehameha was friendly to people of all nations.

In 1797 Keōpūolani gave birth to a son, Liholiho. Later Liholiho became Kamehameha II.

Liholiho, Kamehameha II

Law of the
Splintered Paddle

In 1797 the man who struck Kamehameha with a paddle twelve years earlier was brought before the great ruler to be punished. Instead Kamehameha chose to forgive the fisherman. He blamed himself for attacking innocent people. Kamehameha gave the fisherman a gift of lands and set him free.

Kamehameha made a law to protect the weak from the strong. *Māmalahoe Kānāwai* is the "Law of the Splintered Paddle."

Māmalahoe Kānāawai

E nā kānaka,

E mālama ʻoukou i ke akua

A e mālama hoʻi ke kanaka nui a me kanaka iki;

E hele ka ʻelemakule, ka luahine, a me ke kama

A moe i ke ala

ʻAʻohe mea nāna e hoʻopilikia.

Hewa nō. Make.

Law of the Splintered Paddle

O my people,

Honor thy god;

Respect alike [the rights of] men great and humble;

See to it that our aged, our women,
   and our children

Lie down to sleep by the roadside

Without fear of harm.

Disobey, and die.

Gifts for Pele

Hualālai Volcano erupted in 1801. The lava flow burned houses and filled fishponds. It toppled trees. It did not stop. A *kahuna* said that Pele was angry and Kamehameha must calm her down. To do this he must offer her the proper gifts.

At first Kamehameha hesitated. He thought Pele would kill him. But the *kahuna* told him he would not die. Kamehameha took his offerings and cast them in the flowing lava. He prayed to Pele but the fire burned on.

Kamehameha then cut some of his hair and threw it into the fire. This was his last gift. By offering his own hair he was giving himself to Pele. The lava stopped flowing.

Kamehameha offered Pele a gift of his own hair

A Year in Lahaina

Kamehameha moved from Hilo to Lahaina in 1803. There he lived in the red stone house built for Ka'ahumanu, his favorite wife.

John Young was the governor of Hawai'i between 1802 and 1812 while Kamehameha was away from the island.

1810:
All the Islands United

Kamehameha moved his capital from Lahaina to Honolulu in 1804. Once again he made plans to conquer Kaua'i. This time a terrible disease spread among the people killing many of Kamehameha's warriors, including the great chief Ke'eaumoku. The disease may have been cholera, a disease of the stomach and intestines. Once again the attack on Kaua'i was postponed.

In 1810 Kamehameha and Kaumuali'i, ruler of Kaua'i and Ni'ihau, met in Honolulu. They agreed to place the two islands under Kamehameha's control and to allow Kaumuali'i to continue ruling Kaua'i and Ni'ihau until his death. Therefore, no battles were ever fought by Kamehameha for Kaua'i and Ni'ihau. Now, for the first time, all the islands were united under one ruler. The prophecy of the Naha stone was fulfilled.

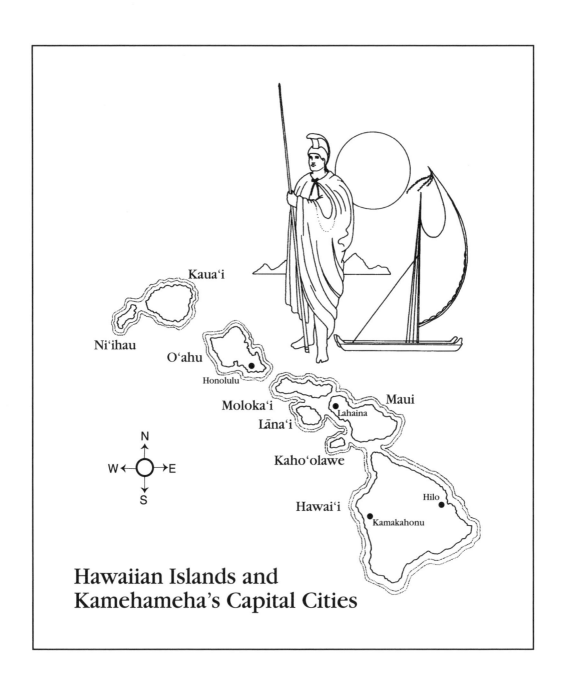

Kaua'i

Ni'ihau

O'ahu

Honolulu

Moloka'i

Lāna'i

Maui

Lahaina

Kaho'olawe

N

W   E

S

Hawai'i

Hilo

Kamakahonu

Hawaiian Islands and Kamehameha's Capital Cities

Return to the Island of Hawai'i

In 1812 Kamehameha returned to Hawai'i to live in Kailua-Kona. Two more children were born to Kamehameha and Keōpūolani. A second son, Kauikeaouli, was born about 1814. Later this son became Kamehameha III. A daughter, Nāhi'ena'ena, was born in 1815.

Kauikeaouli, Kamehameha III

Nāhiʻenaʻena

Kamakahonu,
his Last Home

*K*amehameha spent his last years at
Kamakahonu by Kailua Bay in Kona. He
worked hard as he always had. He built houses and
storehouses for his family and attendants. He was an
expert fisherman and a good farmer. He raised *kalo*
in the uplands of Kona. He built irrigation ditches for
a water system.

Kamehameha raised kalo

Kamehameha rebuilt *heiau* and carved tall images of *'ōhi'a* wood. He rebuilt Ahu'ena, the *heiau* at Kamakahonu. It was an ancient *luakini heiau* where human sacrifices were offered. Kamehameha rededicated it as a *hale o Lono,* a house of Lono, the god of agriculture and peace.

Ahu'ena was used as a place of worship and for meetings. It was here that Liholiho, Kamehameha's heir, was taught how to rule wisely.

Ahu'ena heiau

Foreign ships wanted sandalwood from the islands to trade with the people of China. Because of sandalwood's high value Kamehameha made it a royal monopoly. This meant that he owned all the sandalwood.

Many people went into the mountains to gather the sandalwood. Kamehameha warned them not to cut the young trees. If every tree were cut there would soon be no sandalwood at all. To make sure that did not happen Kamehameha placed a *kapu* on young trees.

Gathering sandalwood

The Hawaiian Flag

In 1794 Captain Vancouver gave Kamehameha a British flag. For twenty-two years Kamehameha flew that flag wherever he was living at the time. In 1816 he had a Hawaiian flag designed. The eight stripes stood for the eight main islands. The Union Jack from the British flag may have been chosen because Kamehameha felt that the islands were under Great Britain's protection.

The Hawaiian flag

Visits by Russian Ships

In November 1816 the Russian exploring ship *Rurick* arrived in Kailua-Kona. It was commanded by Otto von Kotzebue, who later became a good friend of Kamehameha. Kotzebue wrote, "The king is a man of great wisdom and tries to give his people anything he considers useful. He wishes to increase the happiness and not the wants of his people."

It was to Captain Kotzebue that Kamehameha spoke these words about his religion: "These are our gods, whom I worship; whether I do right or wrong, I do not know; but I follow my faith which cannot be wicked, as it commands me never to do wrong."

Captain Otto von Kotzebue and his aides at Kamehameha's court in Kamakahonu, 1816

Louis Choris, the official artist on the *Rurick,* painted a portrait of Kamehameha. He described what happened just before Kamehameha posed for his portrait.

> "I asked Tammeamea [Kamehameha] permission to do his portrait; this project seemed to please him very much, but he asked me to leave him alone an instant, so he could dress. Imagine my surprise on seeing this monarch display himself in the costume of a sailor; he wore blue trousers, a red waistcoat, a clean white shirt and a necktie of yellow silk. I begged him to change his dress; he refused absolutely and insisted on being painted as he was."

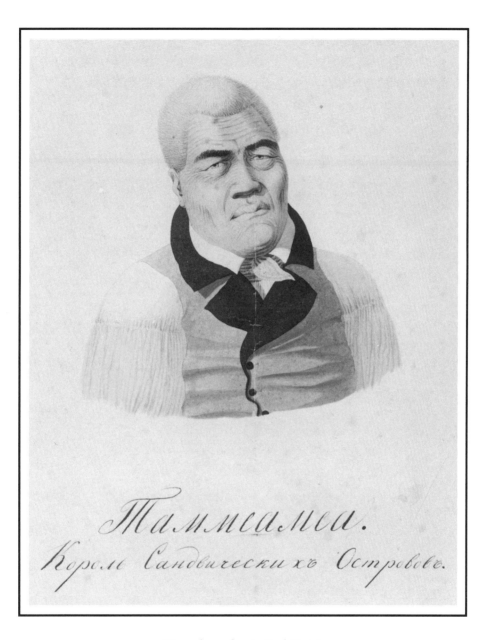

"Kamehameha in Red Vest,"
by Louis Choris (1816)
Portrait courtesy of Honolulu Academy of Arts

The Russian ship *Kamchatka,* under the command of Captain Vasilii Golovnin, arrived at Kailua-Kona, in October 1818. Captain Golovnin visited Kamehameha, who was nearing the end of his life. Kamehameha stretched out his hand and said, "How do you do? *Aloha!*"

Golovnin wrote, "Tameamea [Kamehameha] is already very old… However, he is alert, strong and active, temperate and sober, never takes strong drink, and eats very moderately…. His honesty and love of justice are demonstrated by his behavior."

Last Words

In the spring of 1819 Kamehameha became very ill. Nothing could be done to make him well. A *kahuna* told him that he must offer a human sacrifice to the gods. Kamehameha refused, saying, "The men are *kapu* for the king." By this he meant the men must live to serve his son Liholiho.

Kamehameha's last words were believed to have been:

"E ʻoni wale nō ʻoukou i kuʻu pono ʻaʻole e pau."

"Endless is the good that I have given you to enjoy."

A Secret Burial

*K*amehameha died on May 8, 1819, at Kamakahonu, his home in Kailua-Kona. Before his death he instructed his trusted friend Hoapili to hide his bones in a place where they could never be found.

It was an old custom to hide the bones of beloved chiefs. It was believed that the bones contained some of the chief's *mana,* or divine power. By hiding them the enemy could not steal them and gain control over the dead chief's spirit.

Hoapili, with the help of Hoʻolulu, hid Kamehameha's bones in a secret place. To this day "the morning star alone knows where Kamehameha's bones are guarded."

The Greatest of Chiefs

Kamehameha was the greatest of Hawai'i's chiefs. He kept the ways of his culture and added the best of the new. His people said, "He is a farmer, a fisherman, a maker of cloth, a provider for the needy and a father to the fatherless."

In describing Kamehameha historian Ralph Kuykendall wrote: "He was a man of powerful physique, agile, supple, fearless and skilled in all the warlike and peaceful exercises suitable for an *ali'i*. He had likewise a strong mind... well-filled with the accumulated learning of his race and capable of thinking clearly and effectively. He was an excellent judge of men and had... the faculty of inspiring loyalty in his followers. Ruthless in war, he was kind and forgiving when the need for fighting was past. He had foreigners in his service, ... but they were always his servants, never his masters; his was the better mind and the stronger will."

"Kamehameha, King of the Sandwich Islands"

When it was known that Kamehameha had died another portrait of the king was revealed. The artist Choris had painted a black *kapa* cloak over the red vest. He wanted to portray the ruler as he had first met him that November morning in 1816.

Kamehameha owned the most precious of the long feather cloaks. Its nearly half a million yellow feathers came from eighty thousand *mamo* birds. Tiny red *'i'iwi* feathers are tied to the dark quills of the yellow *mamo* feathers. They are not visible on the surface but they give the cloak a golden-yellow effect. Today the cloak is on display at Bishop Museum.

"Kamehameha, King of the Sandwich Islands,"
by Louis Choris (1816)

Portrait courtesy of Honolulu Academy of Arts

The King Kamehameha Memorial Statue

In 1969 bronze statues of two great persons in the history of Hawai'i were placed in the National Statuary Hall in Washington, D.C.: Kamehameha and Father Damien. They were selected to represent Hawai'i among the greatest heroes of the United States. Kamehameha is the first and only monarch thus far to be honored in this way. His statue is a duplicate of that which stands in front of Ali'iōlani Hale in Honolulu.

Kamehameha holds his spear in his left hand as a reminder that he brought wars to an end. His right hand is extended with palm open as a gesture of the *aloha* spirit.

The United States has honored Kamehameha in other ways as well. The US Navy named a nuclear submarine after Kamehameha. Also, a textbook on great military strategists used by the US Military Academy at West Point ranks Kamehameha with Alexander the Great and Napoleon Bonaparte.

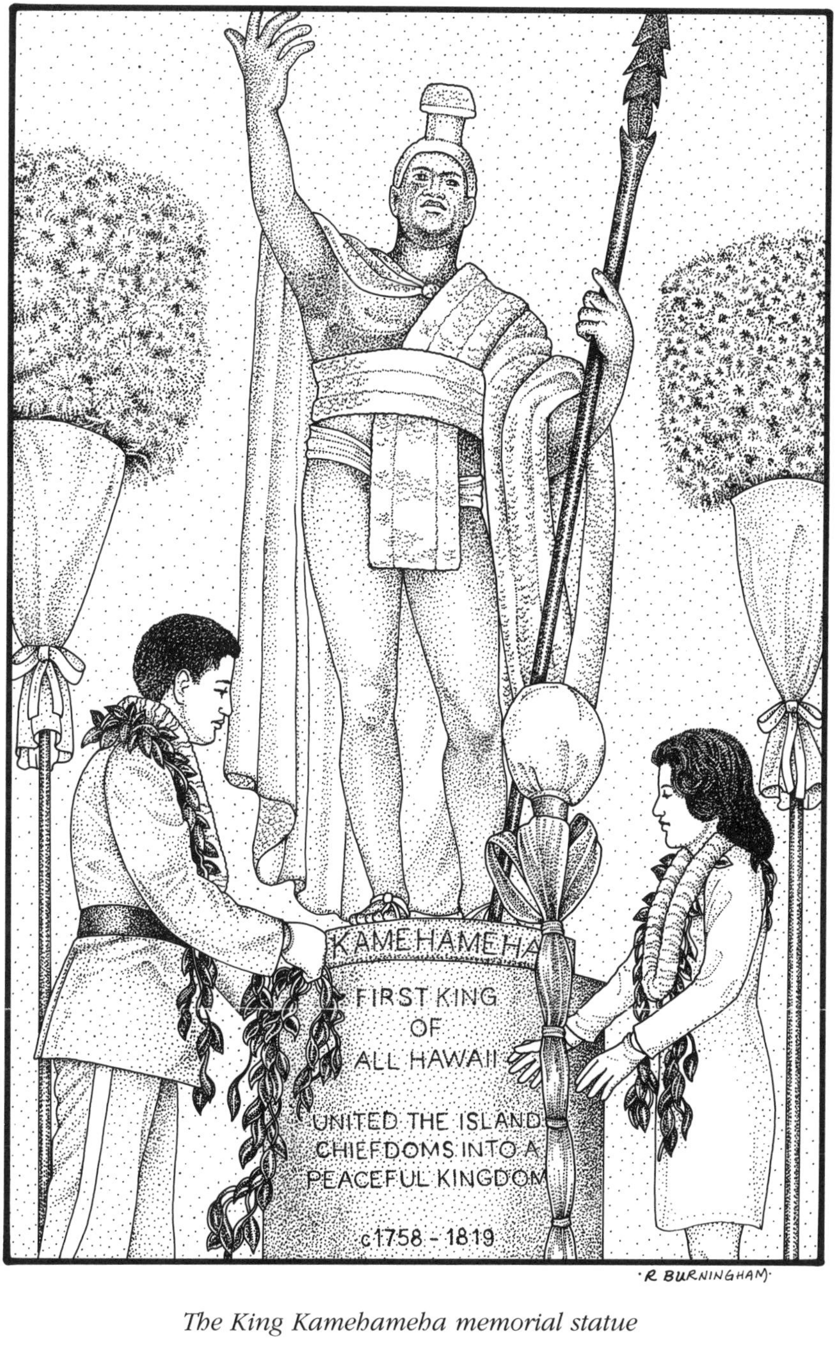
KAMEHAMEHA
FIRST KING
OF
ALL HAWAII
UNITED THE ISLAND
CHIEFDOMS INTO A
PEACEFUL KINGDOM
c1758 - 1819
·R BURNINGHAM·

The King Kamehameha memorial statue

Kamehameha

Mele Inoa   Traditional

'O Kamehameha lani kā'eu ke 'ano kapu,

'O ka haku manawa kapu ali'i kēnā

He ali'i no ka mu'o lani kapu o Lono,

Nona ke kapu, ka wela

Ka hahana i holo i luna o ka wēkiu

Lū ka ōla'i, naue ka honua,

'Oni ke kai, nāueue ka moku,

'Ike i ka lepa koa a ka lani,

Hā'awi wale mai 'o Kahekili

Ua lilo ia kalani nui Keku'iapoiwa i ke kapu,

'Anapu wela ma ka honua mea,

He inoa

He inoa no ka lani Kamehameha kapu ali'i,

He inoa

He inoa no Kamehameha

(Chanted by Ka'upena Wong during the dedication ceremony of the statue of Kamehameha in Washington, D.C., in 1969.)

Kamehameha

A Name Chant   English Translation

Kamehameha is a chief, for him the profound *kapu*

A lord indeed, a sacred chief is he,

A chief from the highest and most sacred realm of
    Lono.

His is the *kapu,* the fiery *kapu,*

The burning *kapu* that reaches the very heavens,

The earth quakes, it is set a-tremble.

The sea is disturbed, the land is moved,

And these are the signs of a mighty warrior.

A gift was given by the chief, Kahekili.

It was carried away by the high chiefess

Keku'iapoiwa, the sacred one.

A flash of hot light over the earth is he.

We chant his praise.

We praise the king, Kamehameha, a noble chief,
    we praise him.

We honor the name Kamehameha.

The Kamehameha Dynasty

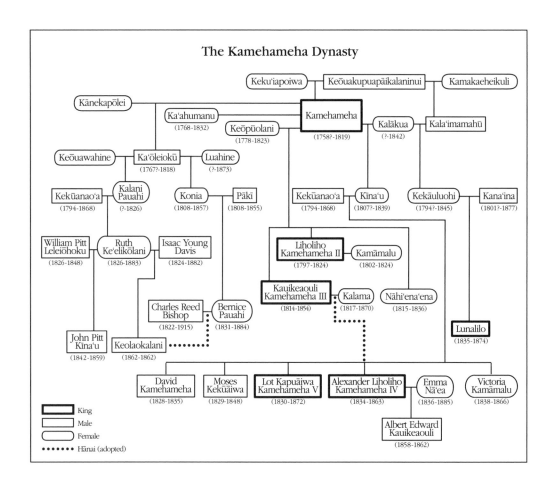

Keku'iapoiwa — Keōuakupuapāikalaninui — Kamakaeheikuli

Kānekapōlei

Ka'ahumanu (1768-1832)

Keōpūolani (1778-1823)

Kamehameha (1758?-1819)

Kalākua (?-1842)

Kala'imamahū

Keōuawahine

Ka'ōleiokū (1767?-1818) — Luahine (?-1873)

Kekūanao'a (1794-1868)

Kalani Pauahi (?-1826)

Konia (1808-1857) — Pākī (1808-1855)

Kekūanao'a (1794-1868) — Kīna'u (1807?-1839)

Kekāuluohi (1794?-1845) — Kana'ina (1801?-1877)

William Pitt Leleiōhoku (1826-1848) — Ruth Ke'elikōlani (1826-1883) — Isaac Young Davis (1824-1882)

Liholiho Kamehameha II (1797-1824) — Kamāmalu (1802-1824)

Charles Reed Bishop (1822-1915) — Bernice Pauahi (1831-1884)

Kauikeaouli Kamehameha III (1814-1854) — Kalama (1817-1870)

Nāhi'ena'ena (1815-1836)

John Pitt Kīna'u (1842-1859)

Keolaokalani (1862-1862)

Lunalilo (1835-1874)

David Kamehameha (1828-1835)

Moses Kekūāiwa (1829-1848)

Lot Kapuāiwa Kamehameha V (1830-1872)

Alexander Liholiho Kamehameha IV (1834-1863) — Emma Nā'ea (1836-1885)

Victoria Kamāmalu (1838-1866)

Albert Edward Kauikeaouli (1858-1862)

King
Male
Female
••••• Hānai (adopted)

118

Bibliography

Barrére, Dorothy B. *Kamehameha in Kona*. Pacific Anthropological Records No. 23, Honolulu: Bernice Pauahi Bishop Museum, 1975.

Bauer, Helen. *Hawaii The Aloha State*. Honolulu: The Bess Press, 1982.

Ching, Francis K.W. and Leonard Ke'ala Kwan, Jr. *Nā Lani Kamehameha*. Honolulu: Hawaiian Studies Institute, Kamehameha Schools/Bernice Pauahi Bishop Estate, 1989.

Curtis, Caroline. *Builders of Hawaii*. Honolulu: The Kamehameha Schools Press, 1966.

Day, Grove A. *Kamehameha, First King of Hawaii*. Honolulu: Hogarth Press-Hawaii, Inc., 1974.

Feher, Joseph. *Hawaii: A Pictorial History*. Honolulu: Bishop Museum Press, 1969.

Forbes, David W. *Encounters With Paradise*. Honolulu: Honolulu Academy of Arts, 1992.

Fornander, Abraham. *An Account of the Polynesian Race*. Tokyo, Japan: Charles E. Tuttle Company, 1973.

Handy, E.S. Craighill and Others. *Ancient Hawaiian Civilization*. Tokyo, Japan: Charles E. Tuttle Company, 1976.

Hawaiian Historical Society. *Paper of the Hawaiian Historical Society, No. 17*. Honolulu: The Printshop Co. Ltd., 1930.

Houston, Victor S.K. *The Hawaiian Flag*. (Brochure) Honolulu: Bishop Museum Press.

Ii, John Papa. *Fragments of Hawaiian History*. Honolulu: Bishop Museum Press, 1959.

Kamakau, Samuel M. *Ruling Chiefs of Hawaii*. Honolulu: The Kamehameha Schools Press, 1961.

Kuykendall, Ralph S. *The Hawaiian Kingdom, Volume I*. Honolulu: The University Press of Hawaii, 1938.

Kuykendall, Ralph S. and A. Grove Day. *Hawaii: A History*. Englewood Cliffs, N.J.: Prentice Hall, Inc., 1976.

McKinzie, Edith Kawelohea. *Hawaiian Genealogies, Vol. 1*. Honolulu: University of Hawaii Press, 1983.

Mellen, Kathleen Dickenson. *The Lonely Warrior*. New York: Hastings House Publishers, Inc., 1949.

Mitchell, Donald D. Kilolani. *Hawaiian Games For Today*. Honolulu: The Kamehameha Schools Press, 1975.

————*Resource Units in Hawaiian Culture*. Honolulu: The Kamehameha Schools Press, 1982.

Pukui, Mary Kawena. *ʻŌlelo Noʻeau: Hawaiian Proverbs & Poetical Sayings*. Honolulu: Bishop Museum Press, 1983.

Pukui, Mary Kawena and Caroline Curtis. *Pikoi*. Honolulu: The Kamehameha Schools Press, 1949.

————*Tales of the Menehune*. Honolulu: The Kamehameha Schools Press, 1960.

Pukui, Mary Kawena and Samuel H. Elbert. *Hawaiian Dictionary*. Honolulu: The University Press of Hawaii, 1971.

Pukui, Mary Kawena, Samuel H. Elbert, and Esther T. Mookini. *Place Names of Hawaii*. Honolulu: The University Press of Hawaii, 1974.

State of Hawaii Statuary Hall Commission. *The King Kamehameha I and Father Damien Memorial Statues*. Washington: United States Government Printing Office, 1970.